This book belongs to

_____

thank you for being our valued customer. we would be grateful if you shared this happy experience on amazon. this helps us to continue providing great products and helps potential buyers to make confident desicisons

COLOR TEST PAGES

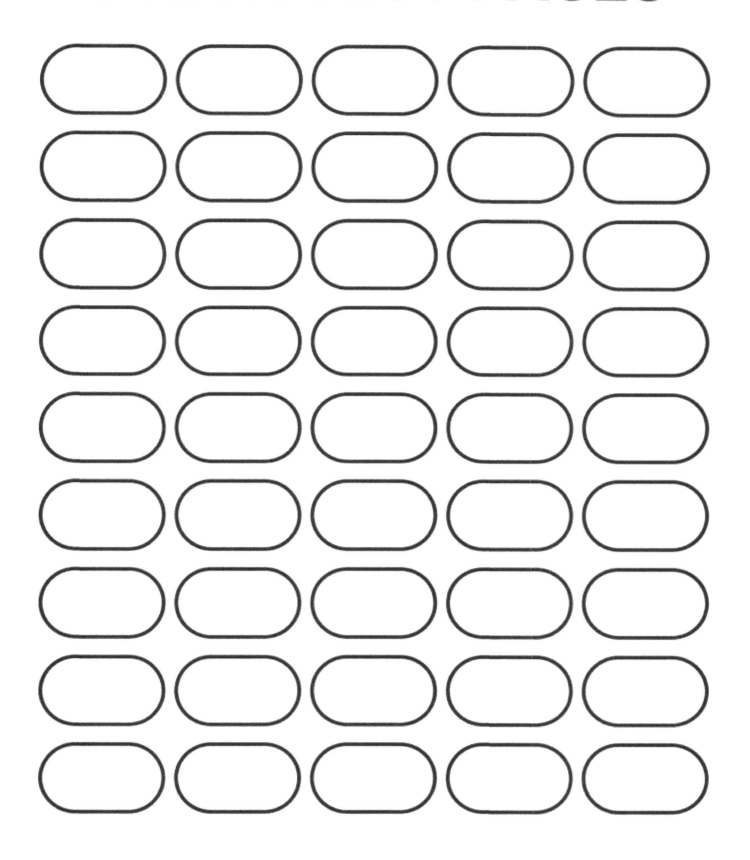

Made in the USA
Las Vegas, NV
22 October 2023

79525836R00046